I0427016

HOW TO SELL LIKE A PRO:

The ultimate guide on how to sell using sales objections and sales closing tips to help you sell better.

Nick Roland

All rights reserved. No part of this publication may be reproduced, distributed, or transmitted in any form or by any means, including photocopying, recording, or other electronic or mechanical methods, without the prior written permission of the publisher, except in the case of brief quotations embodied in critical reviews and certain other noncommercial uses permitted by copyright law.

Copyright© Nick Roland, 2024.

Table of contents

Chapter 1

How to professionally address sales objections

The prospect responds, "I'll get right back to you."

Refrain from saying, Alright, then.

Suggested reply: Excellent, Mr. Prospect. Could you please let me know when you will be responding? or what time would be best for us to speak over the phone or chat again?
· The prospect declares, "I'm broke."

Suggestion for response: I realise that most people worry about money, but will you be curious to discover how I got started or how a student took advantage of the opportunity without having any money at first?

The prospect says, "I need to talk to my parents and spouse."

First suggested response: That's a really good idea. Would it be okay if I assisted you in talking to your parents or spouse about this?

The second suggested response is: Hello, Mr. Prospect. It's a fantastic idea to reach out to your spouse. However, I was just wondering if it meant you couldn't make decisions and then surprise your spouse with an amazing outcome.

What occurs if your potential customer ultimately declines this offer? Will that cause you to give up on realising your (the prospect's) goal?

• The prospect states, "I'm short on time."

Suggestion for response: I know you so well, Mr. Prospect, but would you be interested in learning how to utilise (enter your offer or product) efficiently and accomplish (prospect's want) in a short amount of time?

• Prospect remarks, "The cost is excessive." Don't start defending the expensive pricing.

First suggested response: Mr. Prospect, you made a good point, however, would you perhaps take a moment to consider why others choose to purchase this identical deal from me even if they can find it elsewhere for less money?

Do you truly want something that will help you solve the XYZ problem or something that is cheap?

Second suggested response: Okay, Mr. Prospect. Do you still believe this offer or product is pricey, though, if all it accomplished for you was to enumerate all of your prospect's most pressing issues?

The prospect expresses disinterest.

Recommendation for response: Alright, Mr. Prospect. Tell me precisely what you're interested in, and I'll see how I can help you today.

While nobody isn't interested in fixing their difficulties, this is a warning sign that you haven't fully grasped your prospect's pain point.

• The prospect states, "I'm not ready, but I'm interested."

Advice: If your prospect seems unsure about moving further, try going deeper to uncover the underlying concern.

Suggestion for a response: It's wonderful that you're intrigued, Mr. Prospect, but tell me about the difficulty specifically. Do you still require further clarification on any points?

• Prospect says, "I'll give you a call when I get a moment."

Recommendation for response: Mr. Prospect, I know you're busy right now.

However, precisely when will you be available so that we may resume our call?

Always leave potential clients with obligations rather than wishes or assurances.

• The prospect asks, Is this real? How can I be sure it's not a scam?

First suggested response: Mr. Prospect, I can see your worry, but why do you believe that this is a fraud?

Advice: Ask your prospects about their objections, and then utilise their response to seal the transaction.

Second suggested response: It's quite fair to have some reservations about this offer, product, or company. However, I hope you don't mind spending two minutes looking over this and determining whether or not it's a fraud.

Next, include a link to a picture, video, or page that verifies the legitimacy of your offer.

• The prospect asks, "Can't you give me a discount or lower the price?"

First suggested response: Of course, you may receive a discount, provided that you are okay with accepting the item at a lower price or value (90% will waive the discount at this point).

Second suggested response: I'm sorry, Mr. Prospect, but this is already a discounted price. However, if you're okay with that, you can accept the offer on a payment schedule.
All that a payment plan offers is the option to make instalment payments.

• The prospect says: Does this mean I can acquire something on the cheap after I show results? You'll get paid twice.

Suggested reply: Alright, Mr. Prospect, may I ask you a question first?

Prospect: undoubtedly.

You: Do you enrol in school and complete your studies ahead of schedule?

Prospect: That isn't feasible at all.

You: All right, this offer as well.

The goal is to have your prospect provide their own answers to the questions they pose. If that works well for you, you might offer to assist a prospect in paying a portion of the amount in the meantime.

· The prospect promises to pay you tomorrow.

Suggestion for a response: Excellent Mr. When precisely are you going to make the payment tomorrow? In order for me to gently remind you to stay on course.

• The prospect says: Please email me some details.

Suggested reply: All right, Mr. Prospect, but what comes next? Make sure your prospects have all the information they need about your offer to prevent this issue.

• Prospect says: I'm occupied at the moment.

Suggestion for a response: I completely get it, Mr. Prospect, but when would be the best time to speak with you today? (Make sure your prospect gives you a commitment before you depart.).

• The prospect says, "I know where I can get it cheaper, or I know someone whose price is cheaper."

First suggested response: That's fantastic, Mr. Prospect, but I'm a little curious—are you genuinely looking for something inexpensive, or something that fixes your xyz (pain point) problem?

Second suggested response: That's fantastic, Mr. Prospect. Could you tell me why you came to see me today? When you listen, you'll see that your prospect ends up standing up for you.

• Prospect states: I've tried this previously, but it didn't work out for me, or I purchased a comparable product but didn't see any improvement.

Suggested response: I know how disappointing it is to fall short of your goals, Mr. Prospect, but tell me what you believe prevented you from getting the outcomes you wanted the last time...

Whatever you do, they say, sell them the opposite.
For example,

Prospect states: I received no guidance at all. I worked by myself.

Suggestion for response: Do you think anything else will prevent you from doing xyz? How about hiring someone to mentor you this time? (intended outcome).

• The prospect asks: How much Is it, and what is your fee schedule?

Instead of saying, "It's $100 straight up," let your prospect realise once again how the offer will benefit them.

Suggested response: How much do you believe this offer is worth if it would enable you to get xyz desired outcome without doing what he or she dislikes?

• The prospect queries, "How can I trust you?"

First suggested response: In order to be sure you're secure and making the appropriate choice, what precisely do you need to see?

Second suggested response: That's okay, Mr. Prospect. Could you please take two minutes to look me over and see if I can help you with this or solve your problem? If you have any content on your most popular social media account, please include a link to it.

Third suggested response: Excellent, Mr. Prospect. You may put your faith in the opinions of people I've helped to solve difficulties for, rather than in myself.

(Remove any personal recommendations you may have from people, if any at all.).

• Prospect remarks, "I need to consider this."

Recommendation for response: That's fine, Mr. Prospect, but are there any further clarifications you require?

The prospect says, Let's discuss later.

Suggested reply: Okay, Mr. Prospect, when would be the best time for us to talk today?

• The prospect expresses fear and anxiety. I have already lost money to other firms; what makes this one superior?

Advice: In this situation, you should first express your empathy and acknowledgement of your prospect before outlining how your offer is unique (guaranteed to be a mentorship program).

Example: Mr. Prospect, it's normal to be terrified and afraid. I also feel bad for your loss.

However, the fact that you're not alone in this industry is what makes it great. You have a support group and money-back guarantee to completely remove any possibility of loss, as well as a coach to help you along the way and hold your hands.

• Prospect remarks: However, some companies charge less for the same item?

Suggested reply: That's fantastic, Mr. Prospect, but tell me why you came to see me today.

• The prospect remarks, "Wow, all these?" Do you really think this is real?

Suggestion for a response: Mr. Prospect, I'm curious—were you truly expecting less?

• The prospect asks, How soon will I start earning? When can I start seeing results?

Suggestion for a response: Mr. Prospect, it is up to you. When would you like to see outcomes?

Prospect: at XYZ time.

You: Do you believe anything can prevent you from getting results in xyz time if you follow the right steps and put in the necessary effort?

"I don't see how this will help me," remarks the prospect.

Suggestion for a response: Could I demonstrate how it has benefited others facing similar difficulties as you?

• Prospect says: I need X feature, which your product doesn't have.

Suggestion for a response: Alright, Mr. Prospect, Are you suggesting that's all you need in order to buy something?

If the response is YES, work out how to include X feature in your offer; if not, refer your prospect to a vendor who offers the feature.

• Prospect remarks: It appears challenging and intricate. Is it possible for me?

Suggested response: Do you believe that things will remain difficult even if I demonstrate to you how to use the product in a simpler manner to get the desired outcome?

• Prospect asks: Will I be able to use it?

Recommendation for response: Mr. Prospect, if you attentively follow the straightforward directions and recommendations and take the necessary action, do you still believe that you won't be successful? Will anything prevent you from reaching the prospect's desired outcome, XYZ?

What happens if I lose my money? asks the prospect.

Suggested reply: What gives you the impression that you will lose your money?

Prospect: I've experienced several scams in the past. You should show empathy, provide evidence, and rely on any available assurance.

• The prospect declares, This is a fraud!

Suggested reply: Hmm... Mr. Prospect, what leads you to believe that? (Listen, then draw the prospect in with their response.).

• The prospect says, I'm not sure how this will benefit me.

Suggested reply: Alright, Mr. Prospect, but what specific outcome are you hoping to attain? Let me know how I can support you today.

• The prospect states: Will I still be successful if I don't like networking and can't sell?

Recommendation for response: You will definitely succeed in making money, but only if you are willing to learn how to effectively network and close deals. I think you're okay with it, Mr. Prospect?

Advice: Stories sell! If you experienced the same strange experience, you may be able to tell how you went from being bashful to selling with confidence!

• The prospect asks, What is your profit margin from this?
Suggestion for response: I can easily show you the numbers and tell you that I created them. However, Mr. Prospect, it will simply cause you to believe that the outcomes are achieved with less work.

But you may look at a couple of my and my colleagues' outcomes to see that this is effective. If you have any results, post them now; if not, share others' results.

• The prospect says, Will my business be viable given the intense competition?

Suggestion for response: Of course, Mr. Prospect, but only if you're willing to be receptive to seeing what others aren't doing.
I think you're okay with that.

• The prospect says: I don't want to bother my relatives and friends, but I'm intrigued by this offer or product but I don't have any money.

Suggested response: I know you're busy, Mr. Prospect. Would it be okay if I showed you how to earn money so you could take advantage of this opportunity without bothering your friends and family?

You'll undoubtedly hear "yes," so proceed to tell your prospect about your concept.

What is your assurance that I will receive results from this? asks the prospect.
To ensure success in this situation, all you have to do is provide a money-back guarantee or tight mentorship.

The potential customer states, "I'm a student; I can't afford this." Suggestion for a response: Mr. Prospect, let's discuss this together.

As a student, don't you believe you have even greater motivation to accept this offer and accomplish xyz (the desired outcome)? Would it be okay if I demonstrated to you how you could afford this?

• Prospect says, I'm constantly busy with work or school. Do you think I can accomplish this?

Recommendation for response: I know you're busy, Mr. Prospect, but if I show you how to maximise this offer in less time while still getting the best returns, will you seize it right away?

• The prospect says, I'll pay shortly.

Suggested reply: Excellent, Mr. Prospect, but could you perhaps be more precise about the time? to keep the two of us on course.

"Can't you just teach me straight?" asks the prospect. Is watching the video a prerequisite?

Suggested reply: Eighty percent of those who didn't view the video to gain an understanding of the business before acting are still having a lot of trouble achieving the desired outcome for your prospect at this very moment.

Would you rather stick with that course of action or force yourself to watch the video right now and learn how everything works first?

• The prospect says, I want to meet you in person before taking action.

Suggested response: While meeting in person is a terrific concept, I'm afraid doing business online will be more convenient.

That does not imply that we will ever cross paths. However, I am well aware that trust is at play here. Do you need to observe anything in particular to be certain that you're making the proper choice?

(Most of the time, you lose this specific sale; other times, you seal the deal; in any case, go on.).

• The prospect asks, "Can you teach me for free?" If you're truly making money from this, then why are you asking for payment?

Since your prospect is only uneducated in this situation, educating them is the best approach to sealing the deal. When they receive anything for free, most people won't take your offer seriously.

• Prospect says: When I launch my business, I have no idea where to get customers to buy my stuff. Suggestion for response: Do you still believe there will be an issue if you have someone to demonstrate how to accomplish it once you have access to the product?

• The prospect asks: What is the timeframe in days or months for me to start earning money?

Suggestion for response: It all depends on how deliberately you adhere to the guidelines. While some people saw benefits in weeks, others in months, and yet others in days... Do you now realize how feasible it is to achieve long-term or immediate results?

• The prospect asks, "Why do I need to pay to access this?"

Recommendation for response: You are paying for assistance in committing to and paying attention to the actions required to receive the desired outcome from the product or offer. However, Mr. Prospect, do you believe that this would still be valued if it were given to everyone for free?

• The prospect asks: What distinguishes network marketing from affiliate marketing?

Here, all you need to do is investigate the distinctions and inform your prospect of them.

After that, you may attach a query like this: So, Mr. Prospect, what made you ask the question? Perhaps your potential customer was looking for clarification. If possible, make things even more apparent for your prospect.

The prospect• Prospect says: It is compulsory that I sell items; can't I simply be generating money without doing anything?

This is a completely ignorant question. Inform your potential customer that this is not a Ponzi or investment scam by providing education.

• Prospect says: Can you assist me before I store your contact information?

Suggestion for response: Mr. Prospect, are you still sincerely interested in fixing XYZ's problem or getting XYZ's result?

In response, if the answer is yes, state, "Will you then allow saving my contact information to prevent you from getting this?"...

• Prospect says: I'll pursue something different; I used to be interested in affiliate marketing, but I've lost interest. Suggestion for a response: That's fantastic, Mr. Prospect. Tell me more about your plans and if I can be of any assistance.

Advice: (Keep in mind that your role is to assist your prospect in making a decision, not to persuade them.).

The prospect states, "I used to be interested, but I'm currently employed."
Here, you don't need to persuade the prospect—all you need to do is help them realise that their work and their business are two separate things, and then you can shift the topic to your offer or product.

Suggested reply: I'm glad you now have a job.
Mr. Prospect, you are my hero.
But what if, for the next thirty days, you don't show up
for work? Would your finances still be stable?

Chapter 2

Sales closing ethics: How to improve your selling skills

• Closing a sale is entirely about your prospect, not you.

• To seal the deal, make sure your target and offer are
clear, and most importantly, show them how your offer
may benefit them.

• The discussion to assist your prospect starts at the
closure of the sale, not after the sales process.

• Sales closing is just about assisting customers in
making a purchase; it has nothing to do with pressuring
or persuading them to buy.

• Ask questions, complete agreements, and be a good
listener.

• When closing, show off instead of just talking! Instead
of assuming, ask!

• If you present yourself as a helpful person rather than a salesperson, sales will come to you effortlessly.

• When closing, your tone is all that matters. You should close so confidently that your prospect will think you're an idiot if you reject your offer or goods.

• Always challenge your prospects' objections. Never respond to them.

• Use indirect sales tactics to close the transaction with your prospects.

Employ the EMPATHY effect to close a lot of transactions.

• Educating a difficult or uneducated prospect might occasionally be the most reliable strategy for closing them.

• People who are broke tend to squander time, so target those who understand the value of time and won't bother you with excessive inquiries.

• When asking for commitments from potential clients, use the phrase EXACTLY, SPECIFIC.

• Avoid saying "OKAY" or "ALRIGHT" when finishing a discussion if you don't mean to conclude it.

• applaud, recognize, or even applaud your prospects anytime they decide to do anything or prepare to do something.

• Be constant in increasing your leads to prevent pressing too hard on one prospect; if you are desperate while closing, you'll just come off as a robber wanting your prospect's money.

• If a prospect rejects you, it's not the end of the world. It is not a major concern. You cannot close ten out of ten sales. Nobody can be helped by you. Thus, proceed swiftly to the next prospect if you sense a lack of interest in your own.

• When closing, always address your prospects by their first name; this builds a stronger connection between you both.

• UNTIL THE MONEY HITS YOUR BANK ACCOUNT, THE SALE IS NOT MADE AND THE DEAL IS NOT SEALED.

You've learned a lot thus far, but nothing will change unless you put what you've learned into practice.
Go ahead and close additional transactions.

.

Chapter 3

What are the common mistakes affiliate marketers make?

• Creating leads:

You must create leads through paid advertisements or organic means if you want to profit from affiliate marketing in a way that will change your life.
You may choose to start with organic. However, in the long term, if you want to treble your revenue, sponsored advertisements are the real deal.

• Final sales:

You will lose a sale if you don't know what to say when you're ready to close one.
As an affiliate marketer, you must be able to articulate your offer and brand effectively.
Using voice notes or phone calls in place of in-person conversations is one of the finest techniques for closing deals.You create a human-to-human bond with yourself by doing this.

• Alignment:

Making sales in your profession is all about the initial impression that your leads get when they meet you for the first time; therefore, if your landing page or profile photo doesn't convey a positive image of who you are, you will undoubtedly suffer.

Using your actual photo on your profile and creating a professional landing page are two of the finest methods to establish oneself as an expert.

Every successful business goes through this similar process, so begin by taking the actions that will lead to your desired outcomes.

www.ingramcontent.com/pod-product-compliance
Lightning Source LLC
Chambersburg PA
CBHW071021290526
45795CB00005B/1886